CW00327812

compiled by
Keziah Cooper

"There's wind on the heath, brother;
If I could only feel that,
I would gladly live for ever."

George Borrow

SALMON

Index

Cover pictures *front:* "A Quiet Moment" *back:* "To Appleby Fair"
Title page: "My 'Queenie' Stove"

Printed and Published by J. Salmon Ltd., Sevenoaks, England © Copyright

I AM FORTUNATE to be in the position of embracing two richly diverse cultures. My Romany roots forged my beginning and later life has brought me new challenges and frequently takes unexpected directions.

My family left the roads when I was about five, only returning to our nomadic roots for a couple of months each summer. Nowadays, I have settled 'in brick' at least for the winter season, though, between the rise and fall of the leaf from late spring to late summer, the call of the wild grows too strong, and I live outside. We are fortunate in having a smallholding with five acres of woodland where I can make camp, cook, eat and sleep under the stars – the old habits are too ingrained to relinquish altogether. On the other hand, computers, baths and toilets are the unsung 'temples of convenience' of modern life, so to speak and not to be given up lightly.

I originate from Surrey and have travelled widely over the years, but the fenland landscape in which I now live is where I feel settled. Both my grandmothers passed on their skills to me; from one I learned the arts of dukkering (fortune telling) and from the other the many uses of herbs. Further back, my great grandmothers were both healers and wise old women. Both delivered babies into the world and prepared the bodies of the dead for the leaving of it. I have done these in my time too. Various other family members have been horsemen, gamekeepers and metal workers. Some have kept up the traditional smithing; my father, for instance, worked in metal for many years. From all of these I have learned the Romani patois which is the language spoken by few of the Romany people these days. I have used a little of it in the recipes where I felt it is appropriate and helpful.

As I have tried to portray in the recipes, herbs and flowers from the countryside form a very important part of the Romany peoples' diet wherever they live in the world. The women folk traditionally were always very knowledgeable about their uses, often guarding their secrets well as they could use their 'healing skills' as a way to earn a living. Tisanes and hedgerow 'teas' were used to cure all manner of ailments. As a chavvy (child), Mam and Grandmam used to give me crusts of bread which were green with mould to feed to the grys (horses). They were kept especially for this purpose to cure any infection. Unfortunately, I developed a great liking for this revolting bread myself and, as a consequence, very rarely ailed. Grandmam always kept a jar of jam which was almost crawling with mould which she doled out to any of us with a suspicious cough.

Traditionally, very little cooking is done inside the vardo (caravan). I only had a tiny cast iron 'Queenie' stove in mine and, whilst it could be used to boil a kettle or heat a small saucepan, it mainly warmed the interior of the living area. Hence, most of the recipes are geared to cooking outside. Apart from cooking over an open fire on chitties (the shepherd's crook shaped metal rods) or using fire bars mounted on supports, the other main method of cooking was using a hay pit. This works on the same principle as a slow cooker so the recipes can be easily adapted. A rough guide is that a hay pit meal will need roughly 2½ times as long as conventional cooking methods.

To make a hay pit, dig a hole a foot deeper and a foot wider than the cooking pot to be used and sited close to the main fire. Fill the hole with six inches of hay or straw, although hay is much better. Then, stand the pot in the hole whilst it is empty and pack as tightly as possible around the sides with more hay. When you take the pot out there should be a clearly defined hole. To complete the top, stuff an old sack with yet more hay until it is six inches thick and this will form the "lid". The great advantage of cooking in the hay pit is that it can be left safely all day and will slowly cook the food, allowing the women to dukker or sell their pegs, lace and baskets. When everyone returned to camp in the evening, the pot would be removed from the hay pit and heated up again thoroughly for fifteen minutes before serving.

Regarding the yag (the camp fire), this has enormous significance in the family life of the Rom people. It provides a sense of community as well as giving warmth, light and a means to cook by. It is therefore vital to know how to build a fire properly and safely. When a fire is newly made, a large turf is removed and set a good distance away so that it can be replaced when the kumpania (company) move on. This stops a fire spreading – an essential consideration to those dwelling in tents or a timber vardo!

A large cast iron pan with a lid is an essential utensil as also is a griddle pan or skillet. Unless the meal is a stew, where all the ingredients are put in the pot together, raw ingredients are prepared and tied in muslin bags secured with string to keep away flies and to keep foods separate. Water is added to the pot first, heated to boiling and then the ingredients are added in the order of length of cooking times they require. They can then all be removed and eaten at the same time when the meal is ready. The pots and kettles are suspended from chitties; there may be several of these spiked into the ground around the fire. Providing it is not too windy, the fire is banked up at night with the wood ashes and turves on top, in a pyramid shape. The next morning, it can be quickly rekindled to make tea for breakfast and porridge if it is particularly cold.

"My Vardo"

Creamy Nettles
Dandrimengreskie Smentana

It really is a great shame that more people do not use nettles as a vegetable as they are high in vitamin C and also are a great way of alleviating the discomfort of rheumatism and arthritis. If desired, the vegetable can be served in the same way as spinach with a poached egg on top, for a more substantial meal. We always kept the liquor in which the nettles had been boiled; it was drunk fresh as it contained just as much goodness as the leaves themselves.

A large basinful of nettles   A little butter
¼ pint of either natural yoghurt or single cream
Salt and pepper   Finely chopped fresh mint or parsley

Gather a large container of nettles (wear gloves). Only use the tops if possible as they have a sweeter taste. Wash them well and then simmer in boiling water until tender. Drain them thoroughly and put back into the pot with a little butter and either cream or natural yoghurt and season to taste. Cook for 5 more minutes over a gentle heat with a handful of either finely chopped fresh mint or parsley.

Spanish Treacle Pudding
Zincali Guyi

This pudding is unusual, because I have known it boiled directly in the water and not necessarily steamed. If it is cooked in that manner it has more the consistency of a dumpling. It is particularly nice served with stewed apple which offsets the sweetness of the pudding. This recipe was handed down from a branch of the family who, I believe, performed in circuses in Spain, hence its name.

12 oz flour   4 oz suet   8 oz black treacle
1 teaspoon of bicarbonate of soda
Milk to mix

Rub the suet into the flour (or use shredded suet and mix in) and then stir in the treacle. Finally, stir the bicarbonate of soda into a little of the milk and add this to the flour mixture. Mix with enough milk to give the mixture a soft pastry-like consistency and wrap loosely in a floured cloth, allowing room for the pudding to swell. The pudding should then be wrapped in greaseproof paper with the flaps loosely folded over, tied in a second loose cloth and then steamed for 2 hours (or wrap in kitchen foil). For some reason, it was considered unlucky to cut this pudding; it should be unwrapped and then pulled apart with two forks. Serve with any sweet sauce or with cream.

"The Yag or Camp Fire"

Spicy Parsnips

Vegetables were usually cooked with the meat rather than served as a dish in their own right, but here are two favourites which stand alone.

1 lb parsnips, peeled
A pinch each of ground cloves and paprika   A good pinch of sugar

FOR THE SAUCE

Two small shallots, cut very finely   A knob of butter
A medium curry paste made of ground coriander, cumin, turmeric, chilli and allspice
¼ clove of garlic, finely chopped   ½ pint of good chicken stock
A spoonful of flour made into a cream with a little sour milk or natural yoghurt

Boil the parsnips whole until quite tender and then tear into shreds, using two forks. Sprinkle with the cloves, paprika and sugar. Keep warm by the fire. Meanwhile, gently fry the shallots in the butter until soft, then add all the spices and stir them as they cook; this releases their flavours. Add the stock and bring to the boil, stirring. Stir in the creamed flour to thicken and return the pan to the fire to heat through. Place the parsnips on a bed of plain boiled rice and serve with the sauce poured over.

Parsnip Cheesecakes

This is another useful way to turn parsnips into a simple meal.

1 lb parsnips, peeled
¼ breakfast cup of fresh breadcrumbs
2-3 oz grated cheese (strongly flavoured)
1 dessertspoon of chopped fresh parsley
1 large egg, beaten   Seasoning to taste
Golden breadcrumbs

First, cut up the parsnips, boil until quite tender and then mash. Mix well together the mashed parsnips, grated cheese, parsley and half of the beaten egg and form the mixture into suitable size round cakes with the hands. Dip each cake in the remaining egg, roll in breadcrumbs to cover and shallow fry until golden brown.

"Topping-up the Pudding"

Savoury Leek Pudding

This was a real hard times pudding, but one that we enjoyed nonetheless.

8 oz self raising flour   3 oz suet   Water   3 or 4 leeks, washed, trimmed and sliced
A handful of pignuts or parsnips, diced and chopped
Ends of left-over cheese, chopped   1 or 2 rashers of bacon, finely chopped
A handful of filberts, if available   Mixed dried or fresh herbs

Make up the suet pastry by mixing the flour and suet to a thick paste with a little cold water. Roll out into a circle on a floured board and cut out a quarter segment. Use the main part to line a greased 2 pint pudding basin. Press the edges together and then fill with all the other ingredients. Wet the top edges of the pastry and then fit the lid using the remaining pastry, sealing in all the ingredients. Cover the whole with greaseproof paper, being sure to fold the paper into a pleat in the middle to allow for expansion. Cover with a pudding cloth and tie the paper and the cloth round the basin tightly with string to prevent any water getting into the pudding (or seal with kitchen foil). Steam for 2 or 3 hours in a saucepan, topping up the water as necessary, and serve with a parsley sauce.

Potted Pork
Baulie mas a Coro

This dish was only ever prepared in the months containing an 'R' because we had no means of refrigeration. It tended to be eaten over a period of two days and stored in the pot box outside, at the rear of the vardo, where it was coolest.

1½ lb lean pork   ½ lb belly pork   ½ lb lean smoked bacon pieces
2 fl.oz water   2 fl.oz brandy   2 cloves garlic, crushed or ramsons bulbs
Chopped thyme, mace, black peppercorns, root ginger and a bayleaf, tied in a muslin bag

Set oven to 300°F or Mark 2. Finely cube the meats, put into a pan with all the other ingredients and bring to the boil. Cover and cook in the oven for up to 5 hours or cook in a slow cooker. Add extra water if the mixture shows signs of sticking. When cooked, drain the meat and reserve the liquid. Discard the herbs. Allow the liquor to get cold and the fat to rise and set. Shred, or finely mince the meat. Add a little of the liquor to the meat and mix to a soft paste. Pack down firmly into a basin or jars and cover with a layer of the re-melted fat. This paste will store in the refrigerator for up to 2 days, or it can be frozen.

Pressed Fig Pudding
Maricli Figis

Granda always declared this was his favourite pudding but Grandmam swore it was only because of the copious quantity of tatti pani (brandy) he had with it.

2 lb naturally dried figs	**1 tablespoon caraway seeds**
4 oz whole almonds, not blanched	**3 tablespoons brandy**

Line a pie dish or shallow pan with lightly oiled greaseproof paper. Slice the figs horizontally to form rings, discarding the "tops and tails", then layer in the dish alternately with almonds and caraway seeds. Finally, pour over the tatti pani (brandy) and cover with a final layer of greaseproof paper. Place a weighted plate or board on top and leave to press overnight. Next day, turn out the cake and serve with cream to which a little brandy and a drop of almond essence has been added.

Midsummer Cordial

This was a great favourite at fruit picking time and is a very refreshing drink.

12 lbs of strawberries or raspberries, or a mixture of both.
6 pints water with 3 oz of tartaric acid dissolved into it
1 lb sugar to every pint of liquid after straining.

Put the fruit into a large pan and cover with the water and tartaric acid. Stir frequently, but without breaking or bruising the fruit or the cordial will be dull and cloudy. Keep for 2 days and then strain through muslin (or a fine sieve). Add 1 lb of sugar to every pint of liquid and stir until dissolved, then bottle and cork. Dilute to taste, about 1 part cordial to 10 parts of water.

Date or Currant Fritters

These are very quick and easy to make and were a particular favourite.

4 oz self raising flour   2 eggs, beaten   Water to mix   2 teaspoons sugar
1 teaspoon corn oil   4 oz currants or chopped dates   Oil for frying

Make a stiffish batter with the flour and eggs with enough water to mix. Add the sugar and oil and beat the currants or chopped dates into the mixture. Heat a drizzle of oil in a heavy frying pan or on a griddle and drop on spoonsful of the batter mixture. Cook until golden on each side.

"Fruit Picking Families"

Omnibus Pudding

*This curiously named pudding was handed down by my Great Grandmam who claimed
she made it on the day she first travelled on an omnibus. She was so overcome by
the experience she forgot to buy sugar or bring back eggs, hence the absence
of both in the recipe.*

**4 oz self raising flour   3 oz fine breadcrumbs   6 oz shredded suet
3 oz figs or stoned dates, chopped   3 oz stoned raisins
4 oz golden syrup, slightly warmed and ½ pint milk, mixed together
Ground mixed spice to taste**

Put all the ingredients into a bowl and beat together. Pour the mixture into a
greased pudding basin and cover with a buttered piece of greaseproof paper.
Secure with a cloth tied with a piece of string (or use kitchen foil). Steam for
4 hours. Serve with a vanilla sauce or with custard.

Stewed Eel
Panni Sappor

When we were chivvies and Grandmam used to cook this, we would refuse to eat it if we thought it was eel. We all hated seeing the eels writhing and wriggling for so long out of water. Grandmam used to get fed up with us mithering and say we weren't having eel, it was 'freshwater haddock' that Granda had brought home. Then we would all tuck in nicely and thoroughly enjoy it. It was years before we found out the truth.

1 good size eel, cut into steaks   Milk   Water
1 onion   ½ head of celery, finely chopped   A few mixed vegetables, chopped
Any bits of bacon rinds or bones which would give flavour to the stock, tied in a piece of muslin
A little flour mixed to a paste with water and a knob of butter
Plenty of thyme, parsley, mace and a bayleaf   Salt and pepper

Have ready in a saucepan as much milk and water as will cover the eel. Add all the other ingredients except the flour paste. Bring to the boil and simmer for 30 minutes. Remove the muslin bag and then add the flour paste, stirring all the time to keep it smooth. Serve with mashed potatoes and mushy peas.

"A Watched Pot…"

Jugged Wild Rabbit or Hare
Coro Shoshoi

*This recipe came from my Aunt Amy. She and my Uncle Tom had moved into 'brick'
(a cottage on the edge of a wood) and he definitely epitomised the phrase 'poacher
turned gamekeeper', since he relinquished the former profession to take up the latter.
They kept bees and hens and I loved going there to visit as a youngster.*

**2 rabbits or 1 hare   1 thick slice of bacon   2 carrots, sliced thinly
2 onions, or the leaves and bulbs of wild ramsons, sliced thinly   Salt and pepper
A good handful of hedgerow herbs such as parsley, bayleaf, chervil and dill
1 pint of thickened chicken stock   A little redcurrant jelly   A squeeze of lemon juice**

You will need very fresh rabbits or hare for this dish. Skin and leave in salted water
for a half hour. Dry them and divide into joints. Cut the bacon into neat squares
and place in a hot frying pan with the meat and a little oil. When browned remove
the meat and place into a deep earthenware jar or large jug. Add the thinly sliced
vegetables. Season well and add the herbs. Cover the jar with a lid or a saucer and
stand in a saucepan of boiling water. The thickened stock should be added
gradually so as not to make the contents of the jar lose heat. After cooking gently
for $1\frac{1}{2}$ hours, strain off the gravy into a saucepan and add to it the redcurrant jelly.
Stir until it comes to the boil and then add a little lemon juice. Put the meat and
vegetables onto a hot dish and serve with the sauce poured over.

Ginger Cordial

This drink may be served cold in the summer months to ease hay fever and hot in the winter to prevent colds. It can also be sipped with ice to help bring down a fever.

**2 lbs light soft brown sugar   4 pints water   1 oz whole cloves   1½ oz chillies
1½ oz root ginger, bruised   1 oz cinnamon stick   2 oranges   10 lemons**

Dissolve the sugar in the water over a low heat and then add the spices tied together in a piece of muslin. Bring to the boil and simmer for 1½ hours. Add the zest of half the fruit and simmer for another 10 minutes. Allow to cool and then stir in the juice of all the fruit. Strain and bottle. Dilute to taste.

Sloe Gin

In our family the sloe gin was opened on December 31st to toast in the New Year.

1 lb sloes   1 cinnamon stick   1 lb caster sugar   Gin

Pick the sloes when they are a beautiful soft bluish grey and feel plump. Traditionally they should be pricked all over using a blackthorn from the bush, but a darning needle does just as well. Mix them with the sugar and put them into a large bottle or jar with the cinnamon stick and top up with gin. Cap tightly and keep for 3 to 6 months, turning the jar from time to time. When ready, strain carefully into a bottle and screw on the cap.

Oatcakes

We used to like these with the addition of caraway seeds and a little sugar. We would dip them in Granda's lovina (beer) when we thought he wasn't looking.

½ lb wholemeal flour   1 lb medium oatmeal   1 oz lard   Pinch of salt   Water to mix

Mix together the flour and oatmeal in a bowl and rub in the lard. Add a pinch of salt and mix with enough water to make a dry dough. Roll out thinly and cut into biscuits. Cook on a griddle or heavy pan until pale brown. Serve cold with cheese.

Appleby Junket

This was so called because we used to pick the flower heads en route to Appleby Fair. Elderflowers are a wonderful remedy for hay fever. Grandmam said that nature always provides the cure for any illness. In this case she was definitely right. The elderflowers are usually full out to coincide with the arrival of the sneezy season.

1 pint full cream milk (ideally fresh from the cow)
1 handful of elderflowers   1 teaspoon rennet   1 tablespoon sugar

Heat the milk with the elderflowers for five minutes and then allow to cool to blood heat. Strain the milk and discard the flowers. Stir in the rennet and sugar until the latter dissolves. Leave in a warm place to set, about 2 or 3 hours. Serve with single cream.

Haricot of Mutton

Kerrit Bokra

*This is a real winter warmer. The longer and slower it cooks the fuller the flavour
at the end. It really is worth finding a patch of wild ramsons (wild garlic), because they
have a flavour all their own, a cross between mild onion and a mellow garlic.
A glass of port wine may be added to the stock to give it a more rounded flavour.*

**2 lb joint of mutton or lamb   2 large mild onions
A crushed clove of garlic or a couple of ramson leaves and bulbs, finely chopped
Salt, pepper and paprika to taste   A little flour   ½ pint of stock
2 carrots, sliced thinly   2 turnips, diced finely   ½ head of celery, cut into strips
A handful of pot barley which has been soaked overnight and drained
A handful of haricot beans   A sprig of rosemary   2 dessertspoons of mushroom ketchup**

Divide the chops from the joint (or use lamb chops) and trim the fat away. Cut the
onions into rings and fry them with the meat and with a dash of water until just
beginning to brown (the water will stop them sticking). Add the finely chopped
garlic or ramsons, seasoning and a shake of paprika. Stir the flour into a little of
the stock to make a paste and then add it, with the remaining stock, to the meat
and onions. To this, add the carrots, turnips, celery, pot barley, beans and
rosemary. Set to the side of the fire to cook slowly for an hour or more (or in a
slow cooker). 20 minutes before serving, bring up to full heat and add the ketchup.

"The Peg Seller"

Pancakes with Meat
Bokoli

This was a good meal to make on the occasional day I have cooked inside the vardo, because you only need a skillet and a single cooking pan. If preferred, these pancakes can be filled and stuffed with a fairly dry savoury mince and tomato mixture with plenty of basil and marjoram added for flavour. The soft cheese can still be added.

**1 large egg   ½ pint milk   ½ teaspoon salt   4 oz flour
8 rashers streaky bacon, cut into strips   ½ onion, chopped
½ lb soft cheese, preferably with herbs or garlic added   Lard   Paprika**

Make up the pancake mixture, beating together the egg, milk, salt and flour. Allow to stand for twenty minutes. Cut the streaky bacon into strips and fry gently with the chopped onion until the bacon is beginning to crisp and the onion just going golden, then beat into the cream cheese. Lightly grease the frying pan or griddle with a dab of lard and just cover with the pancake mixture. Cook both sides, fill with the cream cheese and bacon mixture, fold over, sprinkle with paprika and serve immediately.

Spiced Hedgerow Jam

One day Mam was too slow getting her jam into the jars and we all sat around the pan eating it until there was none left. The next time she set my Da to guard the pan.

1 lb blackberries
1 lb other mixed hedgerow fruits, rose hips with the seeds scraped out,
elderberries, sloes, medlars, bullaces etcetera
Three crab apples, roughly chopped
Equal weight to the fruit of preserving sugar
2 cinnamon sticks   Teaspoon of ground ginger

Put all the fruit into a large pan and heat very gently until the juice starts to run from it, then add the sugar and spices. Heat gently to dissolve the sugar then boil hard for 10 minutes before testing for setting by putting a little jam on a cold saucer and waiting for a few minutes before pushing the edge with your finger. If the preserve wrinkles then setting point has been reached. Remove the cinnamon sticks and then decant into warm jars and seal.

"Good Company"

Kentish Hedgerow "Beer"

Granda used to fetch us wild honey from the moors. He would quieten the bees with smoke from smouldering heather and clematis root and then grab the honey away as fast as lightning. It had the most wonderful slightly smoky taste of heather and gorse and was much prized. This beer would only be made while we were in Kent for the hop picking, because it weighed too heavy to travel with. By the time the hops were picked the beer was long gone.

1 small handful of hops
1 small handful of dog rose petals or apothecary rose petals which are very scented
5 pints of water
2 lbs of white sugar or the same amount of honey
20 heads of ripe elderflower clusters. These should ideally be picked in full sun when the dew has dried off them and the wild yeast which will ferment the beer is most active.
½ a cup of white wine vinegar

Boil the hops with the rose petals in half the water for 5 minutes and then strain. Return the liquid to the pan, add the sugar or honey, the elderflowers, the rest of the water and the vinegar. Leave in a warm place for two days before straining and bottling. This is a wonderfully refreshing drink.

Chestnut Pudding

Sometimes I add a level tablespoon of powdered cinnamon to this recipe to ward off coughs and colds. It goes wonderfully well with the subtle flavour of the chestnuts.

½ lb chestnuts, shelled and skinned
4 oz butter or margarine   4 oz caster sugar
4 eggs   ¼ pint milk   Glacé cherries

Boil the chestnuts until tender. Shell and skin them (or buy them ready prepared). Grind them down in a mortar, or in a food processor, then mix all the ingredients together, except the glacé cherries. Halve the cherries and line a lightly greased pudding basin with them. Pour in the mixture, being careful not to dislodge the cherries and cover with a buttered piece of greaseproof paper. Secure with a cloth tied with a piece of string (or use kitchen foil). Steam for 1½ hours. Turn out and serve with a chocolate or vanilla sauce.

Pigeon or Rook Stew

Rooks have a more subtle flavour than pigeons and are more "gamey". Most game dealers don't seem to sell them these days but I have seen them available at game fairs. They are impossibly fiddly to pluck. For this reason I suggest you skin them rather than attempt it and then remove the head and backbone as they give a bitter and unpleasant taste.

4 wood pigeons (or rooks) plucked and prepared for the pot
1 sliced onion (or ramsons) left overnight with a sprinkling of brown sugar
Several large cubes of bacon scraps or salt pork
A large bunch of hedgerow herbs such as chives, chervil, marjoram and sorrel
Salt and pepper   A dash of mushroom ketchup   1 pint of water
1 pint of blackberry or other red wine
Mixture of root vegetables, carrots, parsnips, swede or turnip, all diced ready for the pot

Put all the ingredients into the casserole dish and seal the lid on with a strip of flour and water paste. Bring to a high temperature and then cook in a hay pit or a slow cooker for 4 to 5 hours. Return to the fire for 20 minutes before serving. Serve with floury boiled potatoes. Alternatively, cook conventionally on the top of the stove and simmer in a sealed pot for 1½ to 2 hours until tender. Serve as above.

Skillet-cooked Steak

One of my earliest memories is of Great Grandmam cooking this dish or something very similar, wearing her traditional long skirts and catching the hem alight. Mam quickly smothered her skirt with a dunha (quilt) which fortunately was outside the vardo, airing. Then she applied cold water first, followed by honey to the burns, which healed in two days with not a mark or blister to show for her experience.

4 fine juicy rump steaks about ¾ inch thick
2-3 tablespoons walnut oil, or salad oil of your choosing
2 teaspoons tarragon vinegar   Salt and pepper   1 mild onion, sliced
½ pint good thick beef stock with either home made tomato or mushroom ketchup added

Divide the steaks and cut into 3-inch squares. Lay them in a marinade of the oil and vinegar, then season with salt and pepper. Turn at intervals but allow them to remain in the marinade for two hours. When ready, gently fry the onion in a heavy iron skillet, using very little oil, until soft and add to the beef stock. Drain the steaks slightly, then lay them in the skillet and cook over a clear hot fire, turning frequently, for about 5 to 10 minutes. Add the stock to the pan, heat through very quickly and serve very hot.

"Mother and Daughter"

Raspberry Vinegar
Mura Chute

This was a stock remedy for a sore throat. It was also often eaten with a steamed pudding, or with a batter pudding, as a sweet.

1 lb raspberries   1 pint best cider vinegar   1 lb sugar

Put the fruit and vinegar into a dish, cover and leave to soak for 3 to 5 days. When ready, strain off the liquid into a saucepan and set over a low heat, add the sugar in a slow stream and stir until dissolved. Boil for 10 minutes. Take off the heat, allow to cool and then bottle.

Horseradish Sauce

If Grandmam was feeling feisty, she would add a little cayenne pepper for extra bite.

Horseradish root   ½ lb sugar   ½ pint white vinegar   Salt

Dig up the horseradish in mid-summer. Wash well and peel under cold water. Chop the root finely or beat to a paste with a pestle and mortar. Dissolve the sugar in the warmed vinegar, adding a little salt. Pack a little of the horseradish in layers into a kilner type jar and cover each layer with the vinegar liquid, repeating until the jar is full.

Mushroom and Tomato Ketchups

These home-made ketchups are especially good for use in soups and stews and in many sauces.

3 lbs flat field mushrooms or horse mushrooms   1½ oz salt
2 teaspoons whole allspice   2 inch piece of root ginger, bruised
½ tsp cayenne pepper   A few juniper berries   12 black peppercorns
4 blades of mace, 4 cloves and a little star anise
1 pint of brown vinegar

Sprinkle the mushrooms with the salt and leave overnight. Next day, rinse and drain well and chop roughly. Put in a pan with all the remaining ingredients and simmer for a half hour. Strain, pour into warmed bottles and cap tightly. Stand the bottles in a pan of simmering water for 30 minutes to complete the process of sterilisation.

2 lbs ripe tomatoes   4 shallots, peeled and finely chopped
½ lb cooking apples, peeled, cored and diced   1½ oz mustard seed
4 oz Demerara sugar   1 teaspoon ground ginger   1 heaped tablespoon salt
1 pint vinegar (white or brown)

Boil the tomatoes very gently in a little water until soft and then rub through a sieve or muslin. Return the pulp to the pan with all the other ingredients and boil together slowly until the mixture is a smooth pulp. Bottle and cap tightly when cold.

"A Breezy Breakfast"

Sarma

When I was young we made several trips in May to the great annual Romany pilgrimage at Saintes Maries-de-la-Mer in the Camargue in Southern France. Apart from the excitement of seeing the Camargue cowboys rounding up the wild horses, there was something magical about witnessing so many different tribes coming together in one place. Our aitchen tan (stopping place) was part of a rich tapestry of different cultures. This recipe was garnered from our neighbours there and is one I always associate with those colourful spice-and-garlic scented visits.

Large cabbage leaves (red or green)
4 shallots or a handful of ramsons (leaves and bulbs), chopped   A little oil or butter
2 well flavoured tomatoes, chopped   A mixture of sweet peppers, de-seeded and chopped
Diced cooked meat or bacon (optional)   1 lb plain boiled rice
A good pinch of fresh chopped herbs (dill, parsley, marjoram)
4 oz smoked or herbed soft cheese   1 large egg, beaten

Sauté the shallots or ramsons in the oil or butter until soft, add the tomatoes, peppers and meat (if used) and cook lightly. Remove from the heat and combine the rice, herbs and the cheese into the mixture, including the beaten egg. Fill the cabbage leaves with the mixture and fold them over to make secure parcels. Steam these for twenty minutes and serve with tomato or mushroom ketchup.

Rowan Jelly

Grandmam sometimes used to add a few red currants or even elderberries to darken the colour without making the preserve too astringent on the palate. An option is to add a few, finely chopped sage leaves but only if it is intended to use the jelly as a savoury condiment.

3½ lbs rowan berries, strigged from their stalks
2 or 3 firm apples, peeled, cored and chopped into small pieces (red crab apples are ideal
7 pints water   6 whole cloves   A few juniper berries   Sugar
(a handful of mint leaves can be added – if desired)

Boil the fruit in the water with the cloves and juniper berries. Tip into a jelly bag or muslin cloth and leave to drip into a bowl overnight. Next day, measure the juice and add a pound of preserving sugar to each pint of liquid. Heat gently to dissolve the sugar and then boil hard for 10 minutes before testing for setting by putting a little jelly on a cold saucer and waiting for a few minutes before pushing with the edge of your finger. If the preserve wrinkles then setting point has been reached. Decant into warmed jars and seal with butter. Alternatively, cover with waxed discs and seal with film jam-pot covers. Do not use metal lids which may be affected by the acid content of the jelly. Store for six months before using, to allow the preserve to mature. It is delicious with mutton and any game, with the exception of venison, which goes better with elderberry jelly.

Quire of Paper Pancakes

This was a great favourite but one which we didn't get very often as the cook had to stand for a very long time making endless pancakes; however they do look impressive and are worth the effort.

1 pint of single cream   5 eggs
3 tablespoons self raising flour   8 oz butter, very soft
2 tablespoons of sherry   1 tablespoon of orange flower or rose water
1 tablespoon caster sugar   A little grated nutmeg
Demerara sugar and sherry for sprinkling

Beat all the ingredients together in above and allow to stand for 10 minutes; the batter should be fairly runny. Butter a heavy bottomed frying pan or griddle very lightly and then again between each pancake. Make about 24 pancakes with the mixture. Pile them into a stack on a hot dish, sprinkling a little Demerara sugar and a little sherry between each one as they are made. Serve with cream.

Lemon Barley Water

Grandmam used to make us this as a treat if we went to Epsom Downs for the Derby race week in early June, or to Appleby Horse Fair. It is a very soothing drink for any ailments of the bladder. In that case, a handful of crushed cranberries may be added to the jug.

2 tablespoons of well washed pot barley   4 teaspoons of white sugar
Rinds of two lemons and the juice of one lemon   2 pints of boiling water

Put all the ingredients together into a large earthenware jug and allow to stand for at least 2 hours. Strain and drink frequently in hot weather.

Sarsaparilla

This drink was always reputed to be a great cleanser of the blood and was used as a tonic as well as an everyday drink. Sarsaparilla root can be bought in good health food shops.

4 oz sarsaparilla root   4 pints water

Slice the sarsaparilla root very finely. Put the sliced root into 4 pints of water, bring to the boil and simmer for 4 hours. Strain the root from the water and pound it to a mash. Return it to the same water and boil hard to reduce the liquid down to 2 pints. Strain the thickened liquid, cool and bottle. Use a tablespoon of sarsaparilla to a tumblerful of carbonated water.

"A Camp on the Downs"

Truffled Eggs and Cream

This is a superior variation of scrambled eggs. The English truffle is a rare delicacy, generally found only in beech woods or ancient oak woodland. Unfortunately they are prima donnas *and will only grow where the weather and soil conditions are perfect for them. The human nose is not sensitive enough to scent truffles but Granda used to have a lurcher which was far more adept than any pig at finding these earthy treasures. It was also totally disinclined to eat the prize once uncovered. Granda swore the dog was worth its weight in gold.*

8 very fresh eggs which have been stored with a fresh truffle
A fresh truffle   A little butter, preferably unsalted
4 dessertspoons single cream

First, beat the eggs together. Take the truffle which has been stored with the eggs and pare a few very fine slivers into the beaten egg. Leave to stand for a little while to take up the truffle flavour. Melt the butter in a heavy pan but be careful not to let it burn. When it is just beginning to foam, add the eggs and stir continuously until the mixture is just beginning to set and go creamy. Add the cream, stir again and serve immediately.

Bacon and Sage Pudding
Ballivas Pudding

This was what my Granda would have described as a real 'ribsticker'. I always hoped he meant it was particularly filling not that it gave him raging indigestion.

8 oz self raising flour   3 oz shredded suet   A pinch of salt   Water to mix
1 large onion (or ramsons), finely chopped
A small handful of fresh sage and a little parsley, finely chopped
Lean bacon scraps (smoked or green bacon), chopped

Mix the flour, suet and salt with a little cold water to make a smooth dough. Roll or press out on a floured board. Sprinkle with all the other ingredients. Wet the edges of the pastry, roll up tightly and pinch the ends together in a thick sausage shape. Place the pudding on a piece of greased greaseproof paper on a pudding cloth and roll up tightly. Tie each end securely to make sure there is no ingress of steam and boil for 2 hours (or wrap in kitchen foil). Serve on a hot dish with a white sauce to which is added chopped parsley and silver skin onions.

"Three Generations"

Vinegar Cheese
Chute Cael

Soft cheeses were only made if we were staying in one place for any length of time, otherwise we would buy cheese like anyone else. We tended to prefer the smoked version; Grandmam said it was much safer after Granda returned one night from the kitchemer (pub) and fell into the cheese pit, squashing all her newly made cheese!

2 pints of whole milk (unpastuerised for preference)   1 fl oz white vinegar
Pinch of salt   Chopped herbs as preferred (if desired)

Put the milk into a very clean pan and slowly bring to the boil. When it starts to rise in the pan remove from the heat, add the vinegar and stir smoothly until the mixture separates into curds and whey. Using a piece of muslin loosely tied over a basin, strain the mixture and then tie the ends together to form a bag containing the curds. Hang this bag over a basin to drip for 2 hours in a cool place. Empty the contents into a bowl, add a pinch of salt, with any herbs you may wish and you have a soft cheese. At this stage it can be removed from the bowl and wrapped in blanched nettle leaves and muslin which would then be buried in the ground for a few days, preferably in soil enriched with leaf mould. Alternatively, it could be returned to the muslin from whence it came and be hung high over a wood fire to "smoke" for 24 hours.

Apple Pudding
Paub Guyi

This pudding was a quick standby if everyone arrived back at camp hungry for their evening meal. There were occasions when Granda was so hungry he ate it at the beginning of the meal instead of afterwards! He always got scolded for it, but never took any notice.

2 large cooking apples
A spoonful of honey mixed with a pinch of ground cinnamon
4 oz self raising flour   2 oz suet   Water to mix
Brown sugar for sprinkling

Peel and core the apples and cut into thin slices. Put them in an enamel saucepan with very little water and the honey and cinnamon. Make up the suet pastry with the flour and suet and mixed with a very little cold water and roll out. Cut a circle which will exactly fit the saucepan and lay over the uncooked apples. Put on the saucepan lid which needs to fit well to keep in the steam. Cook for about 20 minutes and serve immediately with a sprinkle of brown sugar.

Rolled Stuffed Pastries
Saviako

Grandmam used to make the pastry for this but she had a knack for it which, sadly, I have failed to inherit; so I use filo sheets.

12 oz cooked lamb, minced or finely chopped
1 onion, finely chopped or a handful of chopped ramsons
A pinch each of turmeric, paprika, fenugreek and coriander
Finely chopped mint leaves   3-5 oz fresh soft cheese   3 oz raisins
A little chutney or mushroom or tomato ketchup (if desired)   20 sheets filo pastry

Gently sauté the onion or ramsons in a little oil with the spices and mint to allow the flavours to blend, then add the lamb and heat through thoroughly. Add to the mixture in the pan, the cheese, raisins and chutney or ketchup and stir together. Remove from the heat and allow to cool slightly. Using the filo sheets, put a large spoonful of mixture on to the pastry and fold into triangular shapes, as samosas. Seal the pastry with a little water and tuck the remaining flap into the underside of the "envelope". The contents will now be completely enclosed. Continue with the remaining mixture and pastry. Deep or shallow fry in oil for about 5 minutes. A sweet version can be made using cooked apple, raisins, spices, brown sugar and a little grated lemon rind, all mixed together and cooked in the same way.

METRIC CONVERSIONS

The weights, measures and oven temperatures used in the preceding recipes can be easily converted to their metric equivalents. The conversions listed below are only approximate, having been rounded up or down as may be appropriate.

Weights

Avoirdupois	Metric
1 oz.	just under 30 grams
4 oz. (¼ lb.)	app. 115 grams
8 oz. (½ lb.)	app. 230 grams
1 lb.	454 grams

Liquid Measures

Imperial	Metric
1 tablespoon (liquid only)	20 millilitres
1 fl. oz.	app. 30 millilitres
1 gill (¼ pt.)	app. 145 millilitres
½ pt.	app. 285 millilitres
1 pt.	app. 570 millilitres
1 qt.	app. 1.140 litres

Oven Temperatures

	°Fahrenheit	Gas Mark	°Celsius
Slow	300	2	150
	325	3	170
Moderate	350	4	180
	375	5	190
	400	6	200
Hot	425	7	220
	450	8	230
	475	9	240

Flour as specified in these recipes refers to plain flour unless otherwise described.

Photos pages 9, 12, 20, 28, 36 and 44 courtesy of Barrie Law, Romany Gypsy Photograph Collection, York